The Game-Changing LEADER SERVES

Keys to Getting
the Most from Your
Employees and Volunteers

DESTONIE BELL

The Game-Changing Leader Serves: Keys to Getting the Most from Your Employees and Volunteers

Copyright © 2023 by Destined to Lead Consulting Network, LLC

All rights reserved.

No portion of this book may be reproduced in any form without written permission from the publisher or author, except as permitted by U.S. copyright law.

This publication is designed to provide accurate and authoritative information in regard to the subject matter covered. It is sold with the understanding that neither the author(s) nor the publisher is engaged in rendering legal, investment, professional counseling, or other professional services. While the publisher and author(s) have used their best efforts in preparing this book, they make no representations or warranties with respect to the accuracy or completeness of the contents of this book and specifically disclaim any implied warranties of merchantability or fitness for a particular purpose. No warranty may be created or extended by sales representatives or written sales materials. The advice and strategies contained herein may not be suitable for your situation. You should consult with a professional when appropriate. Neither the publisher nor the author(s) shall be liable for any loss of profit or any other commercial damages, including but not limited to special, incidental, consequential, personal, or other damages.

For information contact: Destonie Bell, destinedtoleadconsulting@gmail.com

Book Development Consultant: Char-Michelle McDowell (leadwithchar.com)

Publishing Consultant: Sinyon Ducksworth (letthepaperspeak.com)

Cover Designed by Brandon Graphic Designs (brangraphicd.com)

Unless otherwise indicated, all Scripture quotations are taken from the King James Version of the Bible.

Scripture quotations marked MSG are from *The Message*. Copyright © 1993, 1994, 1995, 1996, 2000, 2001, 2002 by NavPress Publishing Group. All rights reserved. Used by permission.

THE GAME-CHANGING LEADER SERVES

Scripture quotations marked NIV are from Holy Bible, New International Version®, NIV® Copyright ©1973, 1978, 1984, 2011 by Biblica, Inc.® Used by permission. All rights reserved worldwide.

ISBN: 979-8-218-20195-1

1st edition

Library of Congress Control Number: 2023908453

Printed in the United States of America

I want to dedicate this book to the leader who wants to lead from a place of servitude. You feel the leader inside of you ready to burst out but need a few tools to fully become.

I've got you!

—*Destonie*

Contents

Foreword #1	IX
Foreword #2	XIII
Introduction	XVII
1. Effective Communication	1
2. Relationship Building	13
3. Power of Accountability	25
4. Feedback vs Push Back	35
5. The Game-Changing Leader	44
6. Victory	56
Leadership Toolbox	63
Acknowledgments	65
About the Author	69
Let's Stay In Touch	71
Notes	73

Foreword #1

by Latoya Johnson-Foster

When Destonie asked me to write the foreword for her book, I was shocked and excited because this was not something I had ever done. My friendship with Destonie goes back ten-plus years, as we met at Chicago State University, where we both were studying Psychology. As undergrads, we instantly connected and developed a buddy friendship. We have watched each other grow from young women who had a hunger and passion to college-educated, career-oriented women, and now married and settled in our careers. I've been fortunate to grow in the field of mental health from starting out as a Direct Support Professional to now being a counseling private practice owner and self-published author. With my background, I totally understand the drive and tenacity it takes to be a leader with a vision and purpose.

I've always known Destonie to be a leader, a servant of God, and a go-getter. I completely admired her strength and tenacity especially given the life challenges she experienced at such a young age. However, she has used those challenges to help her become the boss lady, friend, and wife that she is now.

I've witnessed Destonie work herself up the career ladder and continue to grow over the past ten years. When we first met, she worked two jobs in retail while attending college full-time. She would eventually transition from working at a hospital to now as Dean of Operations at a College Prep High School.

Destonie has been employed at the College Prep High School for the past eight years and has worked herself up from being an administrative assistant to Dean of Operations. Although she has faced many challenges while working in education, she never let that stop her from growing and taking on leadership roles. This book will provide practical ways to be a leader and get the best out of your employees and volunteers. As a friend who has traveled along this journey with her, I have truly witnessed her turning pain into power to become knowledgeable in this subject matter.

The Game-Changing Leader Serves: Keys to Getting the Most from Your Employees and Volunteers has been written by someone with years of experience as a leader, not only in the workplace but in other areas of life as well. Destonie has been a servant and leader at church, in her friendships, and family lives as well. Her love for God, dedication, honesty, and willingness to learn and constantly grow in life are admirable. From the time that I've known her, she has consistently been a fearless leader and not afraid to go after what she wants. The thing I admire even more about Destonie is that she does not make a move without praying to God to order her footsteps first.

THE GAME-CHANGING LEADER SERVES

This book is designed for people who are looking to become or are currently leaders, bosses, managers, etc., in their respective fields. As a woman who's worked her way up the educational ladder, Destonie can provide individuals with the right tools and advice on how to become an effective leader. In order to become an effective leader, you must be able to build healthy relationships with others, communicate effectively, inspire others, think critically, have accountability, be honest, have integrity, and most importantly lead by example. This book provides practical keys to help people learn more about themselves, including the necessary tools to be a great leader and learn how to put action into play.

When you think about how you can become a better and more effective leader in your workplace, use *The Game-Changing Leader Serves: Keys to Getting the Most from Your Employees and Volunteers* as a guide to help you accomplish that goal. Without a shadow of a doubt, I know that Destonie has prayed to God to help her carefully and meticulously write out each chapter to provide readers with the best advice on how to become a great leader. As someone who has put in the work, time, dedication, and consistency to get to the level she is now cannot be overlooked. Destonie's growth was not an overnight success, but a matter of hard work and dedication to become a leader in the field of education.

As I conclude this foreword, I want you all to know that God doesn't call the qualified, He qualifies the called. Destonie is truly a woman of God and I know that the material in this book has been ordained by God. This book is written with careful thought and consideration; coupled with lots of prayers to provide guidance and advice. As a reader, I know that you will receive what you need from this book to make you the best leader possible. Destonie, I am so proud of you for finishing your book and becoming an author! Congratulations to you my friend and I wish you much success with your book.

With love,

Latoya Johnson-Foster, MA, LCPC, Owner—Rediscovering You Counseling, PLLC; Author of— *I Got This! 30 Day Tips for Black Women with Anxiety or Depression,* and *I'm Not Your Superwoman: An Interactive Guide to Understanding the Black Superwoman Syndrome*

Foreword #2

Kashawndra Wilson

I have been in education for seventeen years, serving in schools dedicated to providing transformational access to Chicago's black and brown students. I have been blessed to lead school change and manage results through adults for ten of my seventeen years. I have had the pleasure of serving alongside Destonie for seven years, during which I have seen her growth and evolution as a leader.

Destonie was born to lead and has always had a high ceiling. She sets a bar for excellence and works relentlessly to pursue it, which is why she has excelled in every role given to her on her path toward leading as a Dean of Operations. In her current role, she is leading a high-performing team. A team that is consistent, meeting their goals and outputs. It's a team that is held to the high standard that Destonie sets for herself. On her path to this role, she has had the opportunity to be led by various managers and now ultimately gets to apply lessons learned about leadership to her own team.

Under Destonie's leadership, her team has – soared. She has had the ability to tap into and unleash the potential of all members of the team, truly bringing out the best in her people. Her team is clear on their priorities, feels supported with the communication that they need to be effective, and operates as a unit rooted in service as they support all members of our community. Destonie's ability to lead is rooted in value-based leadership and communication.

Destonie exemplifies our values of results, follow-through, and respect. She cares deeply about operating in excellence, fidelity, and doing what is right. She has been a model of high support and high accountability, never shying away from the conversations that need to be had or the work that has to get done in order to ensure our students, families, and staff have a positive experience.

Destonie values communication and therefore leverages communication in all that she does. She recognizes that people are empowered to be their best when there is clarity, and they are equipped with any knowledge that directly impacts their work. Because of the importance of communication, Destonie has created multiple systems and structures that enable her to leverage its power and has built the ability of her team to do the same.

Effective Leadership is one of our greatest tools for maximizing results. All great organizations, companies, schools, and teams start with great leaders. This is why this book matters. Using her experience and research, Destonie has distilled the key elements needed for getting the best out of the people that you lead, thus changing the game. In this book, you will be provided with multiple gems that will enable you to leverage your leadership, including how to communicate effectively, the power in building relationships while also holding people accountable, and the distinction between feedback and pushback.

Leadership is an honor and gift. An honor that has great responsibility. As a leader, not only are you responsible for delivering on the commitments that you or your organization has made to your stakeholders, but you are also responsible for the development of the people that you manage. If you are seeking a resource that will help you bring out the best in the people that you lead, while also building your competency and confidence as a leader, this is a resource for you.

Much love,

Kashawndra Wilson, *Spelman College BS - Biology/Pre-Med; Northwestern University MS - Secondary Education Principal*

Introduction

Leadership has never been about power, instead, it has always been about serving others. As leaders, we must adopt this perspective and realize that it's a privilege and a great opportunity to serve our employees and volunteers. No leader changes the game by being demanding to their subordinates or those under them, but they change the game by developing their team to be their best self.

My passion to serve others with excellence is innate. It isn't anything I was necessarily taught, but it is something I continue to capitalize upon and grow. As you read and journey with me, hear my heart from one leader to another, knowing we all have room to grow and become better at leadership. One way to become better is to do less complaining and more creating.

I have learned that complaining about a problem has no value, but creating recommendations and solutions are things that make a difference. That's why I've written this book! It's simply to provide a solution with the goal of helping leaders see from a subordinate's lens and understand their desires and needs. To assist influencers with meeting those needs professionally, I have shared principles and perspectives that can be applied immediately so you can see greater results within your team and/or organization.

I have learned from experience that it is not enough to demand from your team's hand and never build a professional relationship with them from the heart. Here's what I mean, when your team knows that you care about them, there is nothing they won't willingly do for you to help meet business goals.

Being a leader, or an inspiring leader comes with a price. There are some standards and foundational things you must understand to be successful. I encourage you to understand the purpose of and the ability to:

- drive engagement

- measure success

- listen to comprehend

- reproduce leaders

- cultivate a healthy environment

- effectively communicate

In this book, leaders like yourself will read real scenarios that I've encountered, which I call "**Real Talk**," in hopes to clarify a principle I am aiming to convey, so you may know that you're not alone. I understand where you are and perhaps you'll glean from my examples so you can apply the principles in this book and make the necessary improvements and adjustments. For example, leaders oftentimes have insecurities which can be a barrier to developing their employees or volunteers. It can also hinder a leader from receiving help from subordinates for fear of appearing incapable or lacking knowledge.

The desire to write this book comes from my first leadership experience in the role of an Assistant Dean of Operations. As the Dean, I served as the operational leader. The responsibilities for this role were extensive and thus required a thorough knowledge of various company processes. I was responsible for all the matters needed to run an entity within a larger organization. At the same time, I was managing an office team, serving on the leadership team, and serving as the primary liaison to various departments and stakeholders. In addition, I was an organizer and put in charge to oversee the daily operations of the company.

I was so honored by the opportunity and more importantly, I was excited to grow as an employee. Unfortunately, the excitement I possessed was drifting away, day by day. I was often disappointed during this first leadership experience because I had dreamed of it as being a gateway to learning and becoming a great leader one day. The kind of leader who creates a culture of open communication, servanthood, and development to meet the professional needs and desires of my subordinates.

Daily I wished, hoped, and prayed for this kind of experience. It seemed as though I wasn't learning and growing when in fact I was. I just had to see it from a different vantage point.

I not only witnessed wrongdoings toward others, but I endured it myself. The pain was much to bear and I often felt like I couldn't take it anymore, only to soon realize, it was for my good. Watching those whose titles ranked higher than mine and enduring varying mistakes, I understood I was growing! God was actually developing and showing me what not to do. I did not want to become the kind of leader I saw and experienced myself. I desired to become more of a servant leader, and so I did. Greatness is often associated with pain, but to experience it one must endure the process.

My process may not look like yours, but we both must learn to gain wisdom from the pain and grow from the sting of it. It's my ultimate desire to help someone overcome the pain I endured and help leaders avoid putting their subordinates through unnecessary hurt, which creates hostile environments. After reading my book, I pray leaders serve from the heart, lead with right motives, and reproduce great leaders for the future. You got this!

merely the exchange of words. It's pertinent to understand one's point of view and/or perspective. This can be challenging in our world today because people can misinterpret things depending on the technology used to share messages. Effective communication becomes more essential in light of our world now relying more on email and text.

Messaging Through Technology

Technology is a beautiful channel or means to communicate and send messages to your team or your peers. While we live in a digital age, it doesn't automatically mean we'll experience a downsize or reduction in phone calls or face-to-face meetings, especially for pertinent things. The best way any good leader can address important information is to call, have a meeting, and share items verbally. This has the potential to diffuse confusion and limit emotions from erupting unnecessarily.[3]

Think about it! One word or phrase can be misinterpreted by a reader, and as a leader, you want to ensure your message is understood properly and in the right context and tone. When possible, I recommend having a verbal conversation when assigning tasks and projects to your team, especially when there are policy or procedural changes. An in-person meeting can help a person or team come to a deeper consensus on a key issue than if members chimed in electronically. It also allows you to answer questions verbally and read the non-verbal communications in the room.

The late Steven Sample, author of "<u>The Contrarian's Guide to Leadership</u>" and technologist said, "Any leader who thinks that a memo is as effective as a face-to-face meeting, or that an email is as effective as a phone call, is still playing in the minor leagues." Let's leave the minors and play with the major leagues, and discuss the different types of communication people often use.

Types of Communication

To communicate effectively is to be able to communicate efficiently by using some of the communication types below. As we talk about the various types, think about the times you may have used these approaches, and consider how they may have impacted your conversations.

1. **Verbal Communication** is the use of words to dialogue with another individual or group of individuals. An example is a phone conversation, meeting, conference, or in-person interview you are conveying a message to someone using words.

2. **Nonverbal Communication** is the use of body language, eye contact, gestures, and/or facial expressions to communicate. For example, a waving of the hand in America is a nonverbal way to say hello or goodbye. Nonverbals can also be viewed as an ineffective form of communication. A person's body language can cause people to create assumptions and believe

they know what an individual is feeling by their body language when in all cases, that doesn't hold true.

3. **Visual Communication** is the practice of graphically representing information to efficiently and effectively create meaning. This type of communication isn't something you hear people talk about often, however, many are visual communicators like me. At times, you may have to physically show a person what you mean. For example, an employee needs to make copies of a document by using a printer. We know that there are different kinds of printers, so you can either instruct a person on which buttons to press, or you can make paper copies in front of them, demonstrating how to use the printer. Growing up, my mother would always say, "talk is cheap, show me!" As leaders, sometimes, we must recognize which step would be best so our employees can comprehend what we're asking of them. Show them and don't just tell them.

Many may think we hear with our ears only, but we can also listen with our eyes. Here's what I mean by that. We've heard this phrase often, "actions speak louder than words," right? While actions are observed with the eyes, they still speak, causing you to hear or understand something. It goes back to the power of nonverbals if interpreted properly. It takes an upgrade in our communication skillset to truly be effective.

In today's society, especially during the COVID-19 pandemic, we've experienced fewer in-person business and social encounters. This can lead to a deficit in the area of interpersonal relationships. Having these kind of opportunities among family, friends, and co-workers are quickly dwindling, therefore, it's very important to intentionally reengage our communication skills—both verbal and nonverbal—to lay the groundwork for trust. This boils down to the following three rules: Be kind, listen, and tell the truth.

Timely Communication

Effective communication is relatively connected to timely communication. Have you ever had a boss or someone who emailed you late in the evening, asking you to facilitate a meeting the next day? Perhaps, you were asked to be prepared to share financial numbers with leaders higher up, along with other information that would cause you to perform after-work research which was not part of your evening plans. How did you feel? What was going through your mind?

As leaders, we must be more intentional and sensitive toward our subordinates and/or volunteers, ensuring we're not adding unnecessary stress to their current workload. Make an effort to ensure that you are not randomly sharing information at the oddest times. Deciding when it is the best time to communicate will benefit your staff or team in case there's a need for them to prepare something for a meeting. Let's look at an example.

Paula, a manager at a company, sends an email to her team at 11:00 pm stating that she will be arriving late the following day. In her email, she also shared that her late arrival is not due to an emergency. This may seem to be an adequate amount of time, however, it is not effective because of the time in which the email was sent. Most of Paula's staff are asleep, and may not check their emails until well after they arrive at work. What can we learn from Paula's example?

As a game-changing leader, we must aim to do the opposite of what Paula did. She should have communicated her message before leaving the office, or any time before 7:00 pm, as most people are winding down around that time and getting ready for bed. I realize that every situation will not be perfect, but they can be perfected by engaging in crucial conversations.

Crucial Conversations

Without a doubt, in leadership roles, you will have situations arise that will push you to have crucial conversations. Of course, no one wants to have difficult or hard talks, but they are necessary and it is what can ultimately sharpen a leader.

There were times when I struggled to have conversations where opinions varied and emotions were intense. The longer it took me to have the talks, the worse things would get, and things would be harder on me in the end. I would leave conversations with the "woulda, coulda, shoulda" thoughts. You do not want this to be you!

One day, I started having hard conversations with my family to build my courage and confidence. I confronted those who I looked up to and who had authority, sharing how they did things that made me feel uneasy. From there, I began having crucial conversations with those on my job, who were in leadership positions. It was in those spaces that I found myself more confident. I was able to have those necessary conflicting talks with those who reported to me, directly.

Real Talk:

As a supervisor, I conduct individual check-ins with my employees. During those moments, they would complain about things such as, an employee not completing a specific task, which causes a ripple effect of another team member not being able to complete their assignment. Or they complained about an employee not helping out with group tasks. In these cases, I often ask if they have had a conversation with the person, and the answer is always no! They don't want to cause conflict.

Upon hearing things like that, I take action by researching ways to help my team overcome the fear of having difficult conversations with one another. I found a book called <u>Crucial Conversations</u> and its authors share seven proven steps that can resolve issues in a healthy way.[4] There are ways to promote effective communication within a team, but as a leader, you must be open to finding the right solutions to maintain healthy work relationships. This would benefit your team and the environment.

Interpersonal exchanges can be achieved professionally and personally if you follow the book's strategy. Kerry Patterson, along with his co-authors, conveys that the goal of the strategy and techniques are geared towards getting people to lower their defenses, creating mutual respect and understanding, ensuring an emotionally safe environment, and encouraging one's freedom to express themselves. If this is your goal while having the hard talk, then you are on the right track! Check out the seven principles you can master and apply to have effective crucial conversations.

- **Start with heart**: It is easy to give in to our emotions, make sarcastic remarks, and make poor choices in the heat of battle. However, there are two components we must consider: a) know and focus on what you truly want, and b) refuse the fool's choice, which involves talking with someone and making them unhappy or avoiding them altogether. Decide not to lose sight of the main goal.

- **Learn to look**: Become aware of non-verbal conversation cues (including your personal cues) that suggest dialogue is breaking down, so you can bring it back on track.

- **Make it safe**: Once you see signs that you or others feel unsafe, the best approach is to step out of the current conversation, restore safety, then resume the dialogue.

- **Make your stories**: To stay in constructive dialogue, you need to manage your emotions, and not respond relative to how you feel. This, in turn, requires that you understand the "Path to Action," which explains why people react emotionally, and why the same circumstances may trigger different responses in different people.

- **State your path**: Now that you have your emotions in check, you need to master the art of sharing your views persuasively. Learn to share your views without offending others.

- **Explore others' path**: By the time conversations turn crucial, the other party is already moving through their Path to Action. Besides managing our own emotions, we must help others to retrace their path.

- **Move to action**: Finally, we must convert the agreement into results, through specific decisions and follow-up.

THE GAME-CHANGING LEADER SERVES

(list cited from <u>Crucial Conversations</u>)[5]

As I've depicted, crucial conversations between two or more people can be facilitated in a healthy way. It is in these spaces where the stakes are high, opinions vary, and emotions run strong. One day during a team meeting, I had my team watching a video I found on YouTube about crucial conversations. I then followed the steps above to conduct the meeting so that everyone felt respected and heard. I wanted my team to get to a place where they could have hard talks with one another when needed, to ensure the growth and cohesiveness of the team.

To be honest, I did not know how this meeting would turn out. Some people are defensive and everyone is not at a point where they can receive critical feedback without being offended. Using the YouTube video and the prompts from the Crucial Conversations book, the meeting went well! Everyone felt respected and left without showing passive-aggressive behaviors, which is something I wasn't accepting or expecting.

At the beginning of the meeting, I communicated that we would leave whatever was said, in the meeting. I also reminded my team to speak with the heart and learn to look, ensuring a person doesn't feel like you don't care about the things they are stating. A person must also be watchful of their tone and actions in order to make it a safe place. You can state how something made you feel, but be willing to hear the intent, and finally come up with a solution for moving forward.

Leaders who have difficulty and the inability to have crucial conversations feel that it will only cause fires, chaos, and tension amongst their staff. Due to this mindset, avoidance is often one's natural tendency, and it seems like a safe path. As a leader, this isn't something you want because it can cause more stress in the end.

However, possessing excellent communication skills is critical, especially when leading and working with employees and/or volunteers. As leaders, we must make every effort to master being more effective and valuing our team's time. As you build, and continue to build a relationship with your team, there's a potential to increase trust. Therefore, engaging in hard conversations isn't something you will avoid. Instead, implement the principles we've discussed and experience profitable results.

Chapter 2
Relationship Building

"Alone we can do so little; together we can do so much." —**Helen Keller**

LET'S BE REAL, RELATIONSHIPS can be a challenge, but where would we be without them in our lives? We are built to need one another and according to Maslow's hierarchy of needs theory, we all have a desire to belong. I truly believe that if we function together, as a team, we would be more successful than functioning in silos. This is the mindset of a game-changing leader.

Great leaders intentionally engage and they don't mind learning how to connect with those they serve. They understand that in order to be the architect of something great and lasting, relationship building must be the foundation. That foundation can start as one type of relationship and grow into another. In my research, I've learned there are approximately seven types of relationships:[6]

1) Networking - involves people interacting with people both physically and digitally.

2) Leadership - relative to people seeing you as a leader where they can look to you for strategy, plans, and decisions.

3) Influencing - includes having the ability to change one's mind, selling your ideas, plans, decisions, and value.

4) Sales - involves a progressive process from a lead to a loyal customer, due to the rapport and trust one has built.

5) Customer Relationship - involves a combination of showing respect to a customer and providing a remarkable experience.

6) Partner Relationship - a working relationship where you manage connections with suppliers, researchers, and marketers, all while sustaining business.

7) Public Relations - managing relationships with stakeholders such as investors, media representatives, industry influencers, governments, and communities.

As you can see, there are levels to relationships! It is most beneficial when you can identify the appropriate level between you and the other person. Let's define this concept and discuss ways we can connect with our teams and/or volunteers, and influence them.

What is Relationship Building?

Relationship building is all about developing social connections. It is a fundamental business skill that speaks for reputation, influencing, vendor partnerships, stakeholders, etc.[7] Honestly, this has always been a strength for me, but I understand this is not the case for everyone. Most people don't know where to start. Maybe you've felt the same way and didn't know what to say to a person while trying to build a relationship. I get it! It can be intimidating, but as leaders, we must learn how to push past what we feel and break the ice.

You breaking the ice has a specific purpose. You must allow the intent of the relationship to drive you beyond your feelings. Think about it like this for a second. When a guy is interested in a beautiful woman, he must push beyond his fears and internal thoughts, and break the ice. If he plans to have a chance with her, he has to step outside his comfort zone to achieve his goal.

Have you ever been to a networking event? Those can be the worse, right? You don't want to look dumb or say the wrong thing, so you stand there in the corner with your hors d'oeuvres in your hand. You find yourself looking from left to right and then right to left until you talk yourself out of the corner and into the game. Listen, you got this. Just break the ice with a simple "Hello, my name is..." statement. After that, see where the connection leads you! You never know, small talk can lead you through big doors of opportunity.

The Value of Small Talk

Small talk really isn't small, but it's a way to build relationships with your team and/or volunteers. Honestly, it has the potential to scale into something monumental, but you will not experience its capabilities if you don't try!

Small talk can be considered a conversation between people who don't know each other. Often times they are talking about things that have little to no importance. As human beings, we can take in so much information while talking to people, but most of it is from the non-verbal cues we give. Non-verbal communication is just as significant as what is being said. A person's body language, facial gestures, tone, how fast they speak, emotional mood, and much more, all matter. Never discount "small talk" because these conversations have a few benefits.[8]

Now who doesn't like benefits? I want to share with you four benefits of small talk, so you can see the advantages of engaging in it and breaking the ice with those you don't really know.

First, it enables a person to find common ground and shared interest between one or more people. *Second*, it improves active listening skills. When you're meeting someone for the very first time, you are tuned in to that conversation, making sure you're not being rude. You're not constantly looking at your phone, or your Apple watch, but you are attentive. *Third*, like weights, small talk has the ability to build enough muscles to conquer social discomfort and enhance spontaneity. *Finally*, small talk creates a foundation and lays the groundwork for moving into more of a deeper and serious conversation.[9]

Research says an instinctive conversation with work teams or colleagues can spark collaboration, improve creativity, innovation, and performance.[10] For some, it gives people energy and it makes them feel seen. Small talk is beyond the workplace, but it can include places like a coffee shop. Psychologist, Elizabeth Dunn, conducted research and the results showed that customers of a coffee shop felt like they belonged and their happiness increased.[11] If this kind of positive vibe can take place when small talk is made within a coffee shop, just think about what can be achieved in the workplace amongst your teams and peers. Break the ice and embrace building relationships!

Relationships in the Workplace

There are practical ways to build and capitalize on relationships. You may think you need to do something over the top, but you don't! It's the small intentional things. The *first* thing you want to do is initiate a conversation. When you walk into the office be friendly speak, and say hello. It's just that simple. As leaders, we may have days when we are tired, but when you can model relationship-building in front of your employees and volunteers, they will feel appreciated and respected. When your team knows that you are someone who cares and values them, they will start letting down their guards and trusting you.

Every organization has goals, projects, and deadlines they want to meet, but who helps to get it done? Your team! The **second** thing you can do is find out what motivates the people on your team. Some may need words of affirmation, appreciation, and encouragement, while others may desire a gift or some type of reward for their hard work. This was one of my favorite tasks as a leader. I would do various things I knew would put a smile on their faces.

For example, I would leave their favorite item on their desk, anxiously awaiting their arrival to work the next day. They would come into work the next morning happy and feeling very appreciated. The joy they experienced brought me an extra level of pleasure and confidence in myself, relative to leading them.

Learning about my employees, and what they like, dislike, and cherish, further cultivated our relationship and built trust. Identifying and understanding what fuels your staff ultimately helps you accomplish organizational goals. Here are some ideas if you are saying to yourself, "What kinds of things can I do to find out what my employees like?" You can create something as simple as an appreciation spreadsheet, asking your team to list things they enjoy. The spreadsheet could include birthdays, favorite snacks, favorite sports, or favorite books, such as **The Game-Changing Leader Serves**, LOL! But seriously, find out what your personnel like.

One last and final thing you can implement is quarterly outings. You or your team can organize and plan after-work events such as WhirlyBall, arcades, dinner, and or an inner city boat cruise. You can even play a word game like Taboo or Headsup. I know you are probably thinking to yourself, "This woman is delirious! How can a guessing game improve my relationship with my team?" No, my game-changing leader, I am not delirious! These types of games will cause you and your team to bond and get to know each other better. Recently, I was in a leadership coaching session and learned that guessing games will humble you. Let me explain myself.

Imagine playing Taboo. You are standing on a stage giving clues, while your team is sitting in the audience. As you proceed to give clues, your team finds it challenging to guess the Taboo word you're trying to get them to blurt out. They become a little agitated and end up complaining. They say things like, "It can't be that hard to give clues for a simple word game! After all, you are the leader and you should know what kind of clues to give!" It's not until it's their turn to give clues, that they realize it wasn't that easy at all. Can you say, *humbled*.

Sometimes the viewpoint from the seat can be very different than the one that's on the stage. Games like this can teach us to have grace for one another, while we serve each other. As leaders, it's so important to understand your employees and volunteers, just as much as they need to understand you. Appreciate them for who they are and what they bring to the table.

I understand that showing appreciation is not everyone's area of strength, and that's okay. However, understanding what makes you, your co-workers, and your subordinates feel encouraged can significantly improve your relationship in the workplace. It has the power to also increase team members' sense of engagement and create a more positive work environment. Authors Gary Chapman and Paul White wrote a book called *The 5 Languages of Appreciation in the Workplace*.[12]

The languages include: 1) words of affirmation, 2) quality time, 3) acts of service, 4) tangible gifts, and 5) physical touch. Let's briefly break these down for more clarity. You can purchase the book for a deep dive into these qualities.[13]

Words of Affirmation - This is when a person uses verbal or written words to affirm another. This type of communication can be done privately, or some people value being affirmed or praised openly, in front of others.

THE GAME-CHANGING LEADER SERVES

Quality Time - People enjoy and value time differently. Some love happy hours, and working on projects together, while some like to know you are being a listening ear.

Acts of Service - Being able to help a colleague with a project or task. It can be encouraging to one because they feel that you won't allow them to get behind in their work.

Tangible Gifts - It's valued when a person is attentive and takes the time to learn what hobby one enjoys, or their favorite food/ candy bar. Purchase a small gift item that's significant to the person.

Physical Touch - In the workplace, this refers to an act of spontaneous celebration – a high five, fist bump, or handshake.

I believe it's very important to know the language of your team because we all need something different. Building a relationship with others gives you an edge, enabling you to quickly identify what is needed and when.

For example, when you've built a relationship, you know when your employees are having an emotional day, or that something just seems wrong. Also, it helps you to see your employees' strengths and weaknesses.

I once heard the quote, "Students don't learn from teachers they don't like." I find this to be true even in leadership. People don't learn or work to their full potential for people they dislike and leaders who don't get to know them as a person. Relationship building is a skill in itself. So, I hope you are asking yourself, "How do I develop relationship-building skills and how can I prove myself?"

Proven Leadership & Empathy

As we continue with the topic of relationship building, let me give you a hard truth, my game-changing friend. A leadership title doesn't automatically get you respect, nor does it cause you to be viewed in a particular light. The truth is this: leaders, especially those who are new to a company, must prove themselves. I recall having to prove myself, but because I understood the value of building relationships, I received respect from my team, without force.

I have worked for companies that tried to make me feel bad because the leader I worked under did not have the abilities or capacity needed to lead and do the job to the fullest. Therefore, it was very challenging to respect the individual and build a working relationship with them. This caused a lack of trust in the leader to direct and guide the team. Cases like this will happen, but as I stated earlier, we must humble ourselves and give grace. Sometimes individuals must grow into their roles and be given a chance. These circumstances are the best times to show empathy.

Empathy is not sympathy. It's more about having compassion and putting yourself in someone else's shoes. I believe showing empathy is vital in any human connection. Being able to understand where a person is coming from is a key connector. When you can relate with a person on some level, a commonality is shared and a close bond may be inevitable. For example, if I am having a rough day, or perhaps experienced a loss in my family, I may not necessarily need sympathy, but empathy. In situations like these, you may notice work being a little slack, or attitudes not being the norm, but as a leader, you should employ empathy. Your response has the ability to help a person heal, feel valued, and feel cared for as a person. So, I believe empathy is a big part of building relationships with your employees. It shows a level of care, and when employees feel cared for, they seem to thrive better.

As you can see, leadership is more than a position. While it's important to be personal, it's necessary to not become common with your team. Take the time to cultivate genuine relationships because this causes employees and volunteers to be motivated and open enough to go the extra mile for you! Take some time to evaluate your current leadership style and determine how well you've been establishing relationships with peers, direct reports, stakeholders, and/or superiors. If you don't know where to begin, reflect on the following questions:

1. Do you and your team know one another's hobbies, interests, personal accomplishments, or challenges?

2. Do most of your professional interactions start with some sort of small talk, or do you generally dive right into the task at hand?

3. Do you tend to only reach out to people when you need something?

4. Do you sense that a conversation shifts when you join the call or enter the room?

5. Do you tend to only socialize with the same one or two colleagues with whom you have the most in common?

6. Do team members come to you with hard questions, concerns, or occasional pushback?

7. Do you periodically have lunches or meetings where you can network?

If you plan to be a game-changing leader, you must decide to build great relationships. John C. Maxwell, a leadership guru, says, "Great leadership is built on great relationships. Those great relationships are the glue that holds successful teams together."[14] I agree, but you just may need some accountability as well. Let's talk about it in the next chapter!

Chapter 3

Power of Accountability

"Check your pride and insecurities at the door because they are the enemy to accountability."

Rules, rules, rules! As kids, most of us hated rules. We could not understand why we couldn't do certain things when we wanted to do them. Sometimes we viewed rules as a cruel punishment, when in fact rules are compassionate protection. It wasn't until we grew up and matured as adults that we understood the value of rules.

Having guidelines, or rules, create boundaries that keep us from danger and harm. Engage with me for a moment and see this in your mind's eye. I want you to imagine a world without rules, specifically driving rules. Do you see people driving in the wrong direction, going down a one-way street? Or maybe drivers are speeding in a school zone where five kids are aiming to cross the street. Considering the things I just described are a scary sight, and a crash waiting to happen, right?

Typical questions often asked after an accident are: "Who was at fault?", "What caused the accident?" Here's the point I'm trying to get across. When rules, guidelines, and expectations are not put in place within the context of a team, who can be held accountable? When there is no measuring stick to abide by, accountability is lost. Let's define and discover the art of accountability; understanding its necessity for all employees at any level.

The Art of Accountability

According to Webster's dictionary, accountability has everything to do with being willing and feeling obligated to accept responsibility for your actions. Let's take it a step further. Accountability also means to ***take ownership*** of your mistakes and fix it when needed. Pause and take a deep breath…If we are honest leaders, we don't always want to take ownership, nor do we want to face the facts. I totally understand how this can be tough, as none of us like to acknowledge when we've messed up or have done something wrong. However, we must leave our pride at the door and be mature, responsible adults. Why? Because your team is counting on you! It's like a marriage. Spouses are accountable for each other and their children.

Although marriage is a beautiful thing, it's a huge responsibility. According to the Bible and the judicial system, a husband and wife are accountable to one another. If your spouse creates debt, guess what? It becomes your debt too. Due to the fact that you are no longer an individual, neither party can tell a judge that the debt doesn't belong to either of them. Legally, all of your debt and assets are shared. When one wins, you both win. When one loses, you both lose. Looking at it from this perspective, it's the same concept for leaders and their teams. Both parties must be accountable for their actions.

When you as a leader model this behavior, your team will follow and trust has a way of increasing. Taking the proper responsibility is vital and beneficial to building an effective and high-performing team. As I stated before, an environment of trust is built and a culture of taking ownership among employees on all levels is implemented. In my opinion, any team that encompasses these habits is a winning team! Listen, accountability does **NOT** have to be perceived as negative, but you can "instill positive accountability" between all parties.[15] If not, it can be frustrating for leaders or those on the team.

During a leadership session, I recalled asking, "How long will I have to take L's! Meaning, how long do I have to take losses for people on the team? After I processed my question, I realized my reason for making that statement. I wasn't trying to divide myself from the team because we know the cliche that says, "There's no I in TEAM." But upon blurting this statement, I recognized that I had said it because one of my leadership peers, who was on the team, wasn't doing her job. They also weren't being held accountable and it appeared that it didn't phase the other parties involved at all! These individuals showed no humility towards the team, which caused me to carry extra weight.

Those on my leadership team were constantly being blamed for others' failures, never taking responsibility for themselves. This weight eventually caused burnout! Have you ever been burned out? It's not a good feeling at all. It has a way of making you unproductive. See, I've learned that "job burnout is a special type of work-related stress — a state of physical or emotional exhaustion that also involves a sense of reduced accomplishment and loss of personal identity."[16] This thing is real! As people with influence, we must be aware of this and not cause our team to feel burned out. You can only cover people for so long and give grace. At some point, we must learn to accept responsibility and embrace accountability as a standard in the workplace.

The Importance of Accountability in the Workplace?

Accountability is crucial in the workplace because it keeps a sense of order and consistency. In addition, it aids the team from being burnt out. Some people will work regardless of who's watching and they don't need to be micromanaged because of who they are. For example, a few team members have been consistently having issues with arriving to work late. It can be presumed that those team members may not understand the value of being on time.

Timeliness is critical and it helps the productivity of operations overall. Like the domino effect, one person's tardiness has the ability to affect others, whether they believe it or not. We cannot discredit people's feelings or disregard titles because we feel like tardiness is minor or not that big of a deal. When others aren't upholding and tending to their tasks successfully, peers can become burnt out for picking up the slack. It's an empowering moment and opportunity to encourage teammates and/or your team to be honest.

Being truthful calls for vulnerability. True leaders have no problem admitting their faults, apologizing for how things have impacted their team, and making things right. They want to follow through with their commitments. Speaking of *follow-through*, that's one of the core values I love about Noble Schools. Noble defines it as this: *"We do what we say we will do both punctually and with attention to detail because the difference between good and great is in the details. We communicate clearly and as far in advance as possible, because our time and the time of our colleagues is valuable. We create accountability by owning mistakes when we make them and hold others accountable to their commitments."*[17] Having a leadership title without the capacity to fulfill its role is a detriment to those you serve.

Real Talk: Read the stories below and decide which leader do you think was respected most and received help from their team.

A) The team was missing information from the Leader and was unable to complete a task. The Leader blames things on the team by saying, "They didn't want to do the task."

B) The team was missing information from the Leader and was unable to complete a task. The Leader said, "I apologize for not getting the information to you in a timely manner, how can I assist?"

If you picked B, you are correct!

Being a leader is a heavyweight to carry. Oftentimes people want roles and titles for which they are not prepared. It's time to be honest with ourselves. We must hold ourselves liable for knowing our own strengths and capabilities. Can you tell I'm passionate about good leadership? I care deeply about operating in excellence, being committed, and doing what is right. As a leader, I model high support and high accountability, never shying away from needful conversations so the work can get done. Lastly, I'm not the kind of leader who's afraid to address situations and call things as I see them. I've learned that this pushes those in my sphere to perform at their best. Make accountability a core part of your workplace culture and experience optimal results!

A New Mindset Breeds Effective Results

As leaders, we create the culture of an organization's environment, and depending on what's been cultivated, one's outlook may be positive or negative. You may be thinking to yourself, how so? It is through our behaviors, habits, attitudes, and what we communicate with our teams.

Taking on a new and different perspective about accountability is a key principle you want to employ, if you expect a high-performing group.

If you had to guess, how does your team, or perhaps volunteers perceive accountability? Do they see it in a positive or negative way? Does the word itself trigger them, causing them to recall a situation they viewed as "not so good?" As a leader, you have the power to change the narrative and influence the mind and how one currently views this concept.

Allow me to share three steps with you, that can be implemented immediately.[18]

Step One: **Establish a positive mindset about accountability.** We all know that one's mind is like a complex computer, however, we all have the power to control it. It takes a lot of effort resetting the mind to think the opposite of what you've always been thinking. If you or your team have always seen accountability negatively, now is the time to reset, reboot, and revitalize your mind. Let's be clear. You cannot change nor do you have control over another's mindset, however, as a game-changing leader you have influence that can cause a shift in mindset, in the midst of your current culture. There will be struggle at first, but consistency is key.

Keep communicating with your team regarding this positive concept. Also, engage them until this type of mindset is established by asking questions such as:

1. How do you view accountability in today's culture?

2. What do we as a team expect from each other as it relates to accountability?

3. How can we display accountability as a team and create this positive shift in our mindset which affects the culture?

Tall, beautiful buildings are not built overnight; instead, it takes time! So, remember that as you work with your team. Have patience and keep communicating.

Step Two: **Create a team contract.** Contracts are usually between one or more people. It outlines specific responsibilities each party is required to handle in order to receive a desired outcome. As leaders, we often lead with the statement, "I'm going to hold you accountable." How many times have you said or heard this phrase? The tone of this thought is less than inspiring, especially because of the negative perspective some of us may have had for so long. Consider this—Instead of you creating a contract, encourage your team to create a contract and make commitments relative to how they will contribute to the positive culture you're looking to build. This can be a time of team building, and they are more likely to align their behaviors to the accountability list they've created.

As I've said before, changed behaviors will not occur overnight, but you can start with the following questions so you can experience success.

1. How do we want to communicate with one another relative to holding each other accountable?

2. When it appears we're going backward and things are becoming negative, what boundary do we want to establish to ensure we get back on the right track?

3. As a team, what are we committed to in order to ensure success?

4. How can we measure our progress in the improvement of positive accountability?

As the saying goes, teamwork makes the dream work. Creating a contract as a team can increase buy-in, causing you to experience the success you desire. After some time has passed, then it's time to assess your wins.

***Step Three*: Assess your progress consistently.** Pushing beyond old habits and functioning according to a new outlook can be difficult, but doable. While cultivating this new culture of positive accountability, decide how often to do a pulse check to see if the outcomes of the team's contract are being achieved and business is being effective. Plan to access and put it on the calendar because as we know, life around the office gets hectic and we tend to forget in the hustle and bustle of things.

In this chapter, we talked a lot about accountability and how it doesn't have to be viewed as negative. As a leader, you have the power to influence your team, helping them drive and optimize organizational results. So let's help to shift the mindsets of our employees or volunteers, and promote this concept of displaying positive accountability. Make the decision to gain their feedback so the team and organization can continue to grow.

Chapter 4
Feedback vs Push Back

"Honest feedback can be a gift that helps you grow!"

IT WAS A THURSDAY morning, during one of my weekly check-in meetings with my manager and *the big boss*. As we were talking, my manager says, "Destonie gives me too much pushback and I don't think she wants to do the job."

I was immediately irritated because I knew my intent was to give feedback; however, it was apparently mistaken for pushback.

Encountering this moment gave me the desire to share the difference between feedback and pushback. It is important we recognize their differences and how we can, as game-changing leaders, embrace them both.

Understanding their distinction can be a great asset to your growth and development, which ultimately affects the organization in which you work. As I explain these concepts, determine which one(s) you can immediately apply.

What is Feedback and Who Gives It?

In its simplest form, feedback is the return of information regarding the results of a process or activity. It's also an evaluative response. Feedback can be given from anyone within a business or organizational context. Some examples include peers, employees, leaders (supervisors), and customers.[19]

- **Peer feedback** - peers who are on the same level, share information in a lighthearted or perhaps brutally honest way.

- **Employee feedback** - subordinates provide input to their boss, and this kind is also known as *upward feedback*.

- **Leader feedback** - supervisors and managers giving guidance/input to their team members. This can occur during mid-year and end-of-the-year performance reviews.

- **Customer feedback** - an organization receives information from those on the outside which can be more constructive.

As you know, feedback isn't always easy to give or receive; however, it's necessary for the improvement and enhancement of any process or specific function of a thing. While we assess from whom feedback can come, let's look at seven different kinds of feedback and which one(s) you can immediately impart to your team culture.

Types of Workplace Feedback [20]

1. **Appreciation Feedback**: Hard work should never go unnoticed. Using this method is all about *recognizing* and *rewarding* someone for their work and efforts. Perhaps someone on your team completed a hard deadline and got things done under pressure. Appreciation is best and more effective when you can be specific about your employee's success. It is most meaningful and motivating, which can cause *high performance*.

2. **Guidance Feedback**: We all can use suggestions on how to improve. This approach gives leaders not just the opportunity to praise their subordinates but to also give advice. You can actually combine appreciation and guidance feedback which leads to a gentle correction that doesn't feel rude. If you make guidance a routine method, it will condition your team to discover new ways to get better.

3. **Encouragement Feedback**: We all need encouragement at one time or another. This type of feedback is an excellent way to boost morale, especially when

an employee/volunteer is having hardship or challenges. Encouragement is helpful when someone is new on the job and it's their first time fulfilling role responsibilities. It motivates them to keep going.

4. **Forward Feedback**: In life, mistakes are bound to happen and it's inevitable. During those moments, choosing forward feedback is best because it focuses on the future, helping team members avoid stagnation from ruminating about their mistakes. It also explains the "why" of an organization's strategy and pinpoints its part in the strategy to achieve. This type of feedback cultivates behaviors that aid your team in reaching new heights.

5. **Coaching Feedback**: This involves planning strategies that will cause the team to win! Using the Guidance and Forward approach is beneficial when you're serving as the coach. It's likely for you to hype up and inspire your workers, which can aid them in becoming more productive, and less distracted.

6. **Informal Feedback**: Sometimes, there's no time for a scheduled meeting when you recognize a spontaneous one is in order. This is the advantage of the informal approach, sensing that immediate feedback is crucial.

7. **Formal Feedback**: Having a routine in an establishment has benefits and employing this approach should be exercised within your organization. This can be set as part of a performance review, or job evaluation. Looking in detail how a team member has been performing and how well they helped to reach team goals.

Each of these feedback types is pertinent and can be helpful to your team and organization. If you're not using any of these already, try one and assess the improvements. Now, there is one feedback type that we want to avoid. Can you guess what it might be?

If you said, "negative feedback," you are correct!

Whether in the workplace or in a different setting, there's some feedback that is just not effective, nor is it beneficial. Quite often people receive **negative feedback** and leaders should really avoid it because it does not increase positive outcomes.[21]

A doctoral candidate, Paul Green, and two other colleagues at Harvard Business School studied field data from a company that used a transparent peer-review process.[22] It gave 300 employees a voice in defining their jobs and with whom they worked. The analysis of this data revealed how negative feedback rarely leads to improvement. There are times you may prefer to give in to the urge of using *criticism* instead of *feedback*, which can cost you. You may be thinking to yourself, what's the difference between the two?

According to a 2019, Forbes article, there are five differences.[23] **See the chart below.**

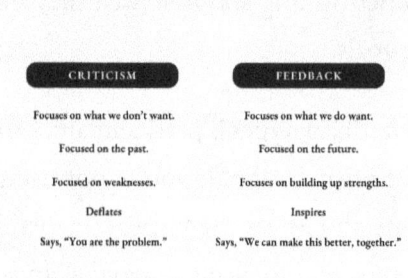

As leaders, we must do our best to get the best out of our employees and volunteers. There are various approaches we can use with individuals and what works for one, may not work best for another. Decide to apply some of these methods shared in this chapter and evaluate the results.

Earlier, I shared how my feedback was mistaken for pushing back, making it appear to my supervisor that I didn't want to do my job. Anyone who knows me knows that I go hard! I am a woman who excels at being excellent and very integral. With that being said, I want us as leaders to understand the meaning of pushback in a work setting and how to have a more positive perception of it.

Pushback Can Precede Amen

THE GAME-CHANGING LEADER SERVES

Webster defines *pushback* as, "resistance or opposition in response to a policy or regulation, especially by those affected." As leaders, resistance and opposition can sometimes feel negative to our souls, whereby our mind is triggered to make us sense that a person doesn't want to be a team player. That person could be your boss, peer, or employee. One of the best ways to determine the accuracy of your belief is to know the work ethic of those on your team.

Just because someone has an opposing thought or perspective from yours, it doesn't mean they won't follow your final direction as the leader. Pushback has some benefits and it provides alternatives regarding how something can be implemented or carried out. As leaders, we cannot take things personally. We should listen to our team members and seek to understand their perspectives before having a fixed mindset. Make room for them to explain themselves regarding their *disagreement*.

For example, employees and/or volunteers may not be saying yes to something because they know they don't have the extra time for extra work added to their *already full* plates. If forced, communication with leadership is needed to help organize new priorities. For example, first-line employees can usually see through a lens best because they are dealing with customers, whom they serve on a daily basis.

Receive It Don't Reject It!

Allowing or receiving pushback has the ability to make you a better leader, in the eyes of your team. They will recognize that things don't only have to be done your way, but you're open to the exchange of others' ideas and perspectives. When you are a servant leader that functions like this, you allow the team to help you think outside the box and achieve goals. And guess what? Your team isn't the only one capable of pushback, but so are you!

Leadership is all about influencing and developing others, which we will get to in the next chapter, but here's why pushing back is advantageous even for you as a leader.[24] As people aim to give you extra work or require unreasonable deadlines for the work to be completed, you can tell them no (pushback).

Here's why I say that:

1. When you understand your limits, you can prioritize your tasks and ensure you complete them with standard quality.

2. When you push back you can focus on leading, coaching, and mentoring your team.

3. As you set boundaries, you don't have to rush to complete your work, which excludes making errors.

4. Your team will appreciate you for limiting extra work

because you weren't afraid to *pushback* with your boss.

Game Changer, now that you know the difference between feedback and pushback use it to help you mature and grow as a leader. We can't be scared of it, embrace it, and change the game!

Chapter 5
The Game-Changing Leader

"My mistake was thinking that I had become a leader because of my position." —**John C. Maxwell**

IMAGINE WALKING INTO A boardroom full of board members that are sitting around the table, and there's just one seat left. That one seat happens to be at the head of the table, in the middle, between members on the right and left of you. How do you feel as you walk into the room? What is going through your mind? Are you nervous? Do you have any doubts? Ultimately, are you prepared to take your seat at the table and lead with confidence? Aha moment, right?

THE GAME-CHANGING LEADER SERVES

Being a leader, and more specifically a game-changing leader is a Big Deal! It has never been about a position, but it is definitely a responsibility that should not be taken lightly. While Merriam-Webster defines *leader* as a person who leads, such as a guide or conductor, the leadership guru, John C. Maxwell, defines it as INFLUENCE. Leaders have the ability to impact others positively or negatively. The question is how do you influence others? How do your behavior or words cause others to become better? Those who follow you are looking up to you, relying on you, and trusting you, so never settle for just a leadership position. If you don't possess or cultivate the mindset and heart posture of a true leader, you are hindering your team from development.

I remember attending a church service one Sunday morning and the sermon title caused me to ponder. The title was called "Prepare to Promote!" The speaker's perspective on this was relative to promotion being purposeful. It's not about being the "big boss," but we should consider questions like, "While in this position, what am I to learn?" Or perhaps, "How can I help my team members develop and grow while occupying this leadership space?" We must come to the realization that the promotion to a leadership seat, whether you're sitting in a seat as a Director, Manager, Supervisor, or Team Lead, is for a greater purpose. Similar to the United States President, it's all about serving the people and ensuring they are being treated well.

Good Leadership Always Serves

Do you recall the quote by Maya Angelou that reads, "At the end of the day, people won't remember what you said or did, but they will remember how you made them feel?" Plainly put, people will always remember how you treated them. As leaders, we must ensure we lead people in the way we want to be led.

How does your boss treat you? What thoughts come to mind when you read that question? If you have bad thoughts about how your boss treats you, then it should cause you to think about how you can do the opposite to ensure you don't mistreat those you lead.

Forbes Magazine shared this quote, **"Becoming a 'good leader' starts with how you treat your team."**[25] I believe this quote to be true, as in life, how we treat people, ranks high. To be a strong and successful leader, it is smart to be flexible and add various leadership types like democratic, autocratic, strategic, transformational, and transactional to your leadership style. Utilizing these styles can help the success of your organization because your team consists of unique individuals who learn and adapt differently to reach common goals. To be honest, good leadership can change, as it is really determined or established in the hearts of your team and their productivity.[26] In addition to treating your team right, you must have an open mind.

The indicator of a strong leader is one who is willing to listen and learn from their team. Being open and aware of other individuals' strengths and weaknesses provides an opportunity to complement one another. Perfection is not the goal; however, building an incredible team that moves with great momentum and dominates tasks, warrants success. This only adds to my point of leadership being more than a spot in high places.

John C. Maxwell says it like this, "leadership is not a noun, it's a verb. It's active. It's movement."[27] This is a good quote and oh so true. I found myself saying something very similar: *Just because a person has a title, it doesn't make them a leader!* When we change our perspective, our behavior also begins to change. High titles mean bigger assignments which means more tasks. You have to do the work!

Before taking or accepting a title, I want to encourage you to search within yourself. Then ask yourself three questions:

- Do I have what it takes to lead in the spirit of excellence?

- Am I flexible and willing to learn what I do not know?

- Do I have an open mind and can I handle others' strengths on my team?

Answering these questions and being honest with yourself will benefit you greatly! I guarantee that you'll see a difference in your leadership approach and so will your team. When Leaders understand the call of a Leader they began to pursue the duty of serving others. Examine yourself and realize what you've been chosen to do.

I have worked under and laterally with people who didn't have the aptitude of a leader. They were not willing to put in the work to become one either. Due to personal insecurities, those individuals weren't able to handle critical feedback, which we often called "adjusting feedback." I can hear you thinking as you're reading this! Yes, you're correct, personal insecurities can lead to an intense environment at the office. I want to see YOU, Leader, YES YOU, lead with confidence. I'm encouraging you to do whatever it takes. Don't be afraid!

Born or Made?

I know we often hear this cliché that some people are born leaders, but it's true! Some people are born leaders and they simply develop as they mature in life. Do you remember when you were a kid and had that friend or classmate who was always bossing people around?!? If you don't remember, then you were probably the bossy friend (LOL)! Those who are commonly seen as bossy are born leaders. They have an inherent ability in which they don't need to be trained. With or without a title, they manage to lead in some capacity. For example, you see them leading and organizing things for their family, friend groups, and any organization they may be a part of.

Why? Because it's what they were born to do and it comes to them naturally. They don't even have to think about it.

Just a leadership tip: Although you have inherent and ingrained abilities, it would still behoove you to train and continually grow your skills.

"True leadership cannot be awarded, appointed, or assigned. It comes only from influence, and that cannot be mandated. It must be earned. The only thing a title can buy is a little time either to increase your level of influence with others or to undermine it." - John C. Maxwell

Real Talk

In my leadership role, I was considered the middleman who facilitated interaction between stakeholders. I was under poor leadership while training to be a good leader to those under me. I couldn't go to my leader for strategies or development because they didn't have the skills.

One day I was frustrated and complained saying, "How did this person get hired!" I badly desired development, but my leader didn't have the skill sets to help me grow. I felt doomed. To my surprise, the person I spoke to said, "You know you can learn even when you're not being taught. Start looking at what they are not doing and learn from that." It seems crazy, right, but it was so profound and true.

Areas in which my boss lacked competence, I wanted to develop and thrive in those spaces. Therefore, I would push myself to do the opposite. It was from that experience that I began to learn and grow.

Assignments that weren't completed, I would complete them, and by doing that, I was able to learn new skills and become knowledgeable about different roles. Things that I knew were unprofessional or poor communication skills; I would over-communicate because I knew that I wanted to lead well. What am I emphasizing? The importance here is that you can learn even when your leader doesn't have the skill set to teach. You will have to pay attention and put in a little extra work. But it's ok, you got this!

When it was my turn to lead, I had employees who did not seem committed and I needed a strategy of buy-in. One day this thought came to my mind of how I could hold myself accountable. I began asking myself some questions and answered them honestly. The results of my answers, were all YES. To achieve my goal, I brought those same questions into my individual meetings. Asking my team members the same eight questions in relation to their opinion of me.

I would say, for example, "I have a few questions I want to ask you about me, so please answer them honestly."

They would do the exercise and all of their answers, regarding me, would be, *Yes*. Then I'd ask them to answer the same questions about themselves. The goal here was to help my team see that I'm not requiring something of them that I'm not doing myself, as their leader.

Then I'd follow up with, "So when I ask you to be on time, to be a team player, and to be committed, there should be no issue with putting forth the effort to meet the standard, right?"

Their response would be, "Yes, you're right."

It seems so simple, but it's really a profound experience when put into intentional action. I am leading by example and reciprocity is strongly desired from my team.

Here are My Buy-in Questions:

1. Am I a timely Leader?

Yes/No

2. Am I a team player?

Yes/No

3. Do I follow through on what I say?

Yes/No

4. Do I seem to be committed to this work?

Yes/No

5. Do I support the team?

Yes/No

6. Am I punctual for special events or additional events?

Yes/No

7. Do I demand justice and equity for the team?

Yes/No

8. What else do you need from me as a Leader?

Being the change you want to see is all a part of leadership. Things must first begin with you. Of course, it is not a good idea to let your team take control; however, you must be open to hearing other perspectives and thoughts that are in the room. Remember, if you become too rigid and unyielding in your approach, you could be missing out on a wealth of unrealized talent and untapped potential. Each employee carries with them the potential for fresh and different ideas. There could be amazing innovations that can take your operation to an entirely new level. Be open. Despite the leadership approach you desire to use, don't ever forget that you are the manager/supervisor, and you are there as a guide.

Christine Cain, a televangelist, says it like this: *Be the example. Your credibility is our leadership currency. So you must be personally willing to do what you are asking of others.*[28]

Changing You, Changes the Game

Change the game, Leader, AND let Leadership change you. I personally have an Achievement-oriented, fast-paced, organized work style. I like things done in order and on time. You may be asking yourself, "What is Achievement- oriented style?" I am glad you asked.

> *Achievement Orientation is an Emotional Intelligence competency that usually involves one striving to meet or exceed a standard of excellence, welcoming feedback, and continually seeking to improve." A person with this skill is able to balance their own personal drive with the needs of the organization. To obtain that, self-management, relationship management, and understanding the context of any situation is needed.*[29]

As Leaders, we know that Achievement Orientation is not how everyone operates. I tell people, "Wait until you get married or have children because you will learn a lot about yourself."

It's the same with leadership. When you become a leader, people have a way of ensuring you see your flaws and recognize areas of growth. It may seem negative or harsh, but even this could work out for your good. Be willing to learn and grow, and not just be concerned about a title. I may sound redundant, but titles often come with an ego trip if you are not cognizant and ready to check yourself.

While leading within a particular organization, most things went well, but I had a thought. What do you do when you take on poorly managed employees, and they play both sides? They fight or disagree so that they will benefit from the situation. They wear masks, showing two characters and doing so in a deceitful manner to satisfy their personal interests or agenda because they didn't want you as their leader. What do you do when they continue to exude poor performance because they haven't been held accountable prior to your leadership? You remain professional and courteous.

Working with individuals who want to make life difficult for you only make matters worse for themselves. You won't always be able to help everyone because there will always be some people that are okay with mediocrity. There will always be those who want to finesse systems. It may be a lot of work for you to have to continually have follow-up conversations, micromanage them for a while, and continue to go through written warnings for employee performance reviews. However, in the end, you would have helped that employee build skills they didn't previously have or helped them begin searching for a role that would better suit their skill set or desires. Always remember these situations do not constitute you as a poor leader, but these situations are to build your character and strengthen you as you continue to grow and lead.

Promotion is a process. Be determined to go through the process WELL because this is where you will gain victory.

Chapter 6
Victory

"There is always joy at the end if you don't give up. You do know that rain helps seeds to grow!"

WINS AREN'T NECESSARY WITHOUT a battle, and opposition is the prerequisite for any victory. Therefore, the master key to the life of a game-changing leader is never giving up. Yes, there will be some challenges and difficulties, but you must recognize them as a means to mature you. There are two types of leaders, one who refuses to give up and one who gives up during difficult situations. The question is which are you?

John Maxwell created "21 Laws of Leadership" and one of the laws is called The Law of Victory.[30] This law is all about leaders possessing an unwillingness to accept defeat. There is no other alternative to winning. Great leaders always find a way to win. Yes, crises and/or challenges will occur and they can bring out the best or worst in leaders. Things will surface and show you what's in you. This law isn't leader based, instead, it's team-based.

THE GAME-CHANGING LEADER SERVES

The Law of Victory considers the team and how leaders always find a way to win. When you think of a winning team, who comes to mind? Being from Chicago, I think about Michael Jordan and the Chicago Bulls. We all know that Jordan is an amazing leader; however, he still needed his team to win six back-to-back championships in the 90s. If you've ever watched the Netflix documentary, *The Last Dance*, you witnessed his character and how he refused to be defeated. He took ownership if they lost a game and made sure they did what it took to prepare to win the next game. As a game-changing leader, you must do the same. You have to acknowledge the situation you may be faced with but be determined to find a way for you and your team to win. There are three components of victory game-changing leaders must consider.

They are as follows:[31]

1. **Unity of Vision** - A team can only succeed when you have a unified vision. You cannot succeed with potential and talent alone, but everyone must share a common goal, relative to the team, and not an individual.

2. **Diversity of Skills** - Every organization or non-profit needs a variety of skill sets and strengths on a team. As a leader, you must realize that every person has something to contribute to your team.

3. **A Leader Dedicated to Victory and Raising Players to their Potential** - While your team may be diverse with skills, it takes the right leader to help them maximize their potential.

As you lead your team, consider applying these three components and expect a champion team regardless of the challenges you may face.

Real Talk

I acquired a team that had been poorly managed and aspects of the team weren't managed at all! This team was accustomed to doing the bare minimum because they had little to no respect for their prior supervisor, although that person held 'the title' to lead. Once I came on the scene, I took action, creating a team culture and recreating an environment conducive to supporting a true team. With determination, I would alleviate the toxic energy and behaviors by creating several accountability systems.

Every organization needs a system and without it, success can't be expected. As I talked about accountability earlier, I needed to put a system in place when taking on this new team so that each person understood their role on various projects. Using a new process, trust could develop amongst the team. It was also necessary they knew I held no favorites in the spirit of nurturing that trust. You see, we are all responsible for our part.

THE GAME-CHANGING LEADER SERVES

I pushed the team to own all of their tasks and allowed them to present their expertise in front of the staff. Speaking in front of other leaders was developing their confidence. I aim to model leadership in front of my team, and function in excellence, hoping my influence will encourage them to do the same. This is never easy, but the result is always worth it.

Leadership can be challenging, but if you hang in there long enough you will eventually see victory. How do I know? Because it happened to me. What I just shared regarding the team I ended up inheriting and taking on extra assignments for over one year, lead to an official leadership position! I was given a salary, and additionally a bonus to reward the extra work I was doing before receiving 'a title'. I went from managing three people to five people to eight people, which reminds me of a scripture found in Luke 12:48 (NIV): *"From everyone who has been given much, much will be demanded; and from the one who has been entrusted with much, much more will be asked."*

I was never looking for a title, but when you do the work the title(s) will come. Someone told me that one day and it didn't quite land with me initially. I realize the accuracy of the statement now. All I wanted to do was grow and develop as a leader, so I guess you can say that *I understood the assignment*!

Anytime you're given tasks or called to an assignment believe that you're equipped for the job at hand. Just because you're equipped, it doesn't mean it will be easy or painless. In my pursuit of learning to be the leader I knew I was from within, I quickly realized that it didn't come without the cost of pain. However, I now understand there is purpose in pain. For example, when I started writing this book, I started writing from a place of pain because I didn't want anyone else to endure agony without the proper tools to help navigate through it. I am proud to say that I am completing this book in a season of victory! Looking back, those days of frustration changed my life and mindset of how I viewed leadership. This experience has pushed me in becoming the effective leader I've always envisioned. I remain teachable and I keep staying knowledgeable about my craft.

As a game-changing leader, remaining on the cutting edge will keep you sharp, enabling you to lead your team with confidence, and ultimately helping your organization be profitable. We are consistently victorious because we don't forget to exude the traits that mark us as great leaders:

- Integrity

- Loyalty

- Great personality

- Self-awareness

- Hard-worker

- Tenacious

THE GAME-CHANGING LEADER SERVES

- Love people

Continue serving and putting your feet in the mud with your team. Always understand that no one is perfect, and you just may have to take the heat for your team. The plans you create may not always work out, but it doesn't mean it was pointless. Change your perspective, realize you were at least prepared, and there's always purpose in the process.

After going through a process and enduring three years of poor leadership, I left a company with a *Leadership Award of Excellence*, which to me meant, job well done! You would think receiving the award was the best part, right? Wrong! For me, the best part was that I could see the leadership multiplication principle in action. I reproduced other great leaders. If you're not reproducing others, then what are you really doing?

Please repeat after me: ***"I am now a game-changer because I am the element that comes with leadership (influence), contributing to a result or outcome that changes the existing situation or activity in a significant way."***[32]

Leader, I leave you confidently knowing you got this. Now, GO CHANGE THE LEADERSHIP GAME!!!

Leadership Toolbox

Affirmations & Quotes

(You'll need something to remind you that you got this!)

- Remember, you are unique, and this is your opportunity to create your own definition of a "good leader" (Forbes).

- "Leadership influence (fame) and service...We have to do the work, you have to become a student of your craft" (TLC Center).

- There is always joy at the end if you don't give up. You do know that rain helps seeds to grow!!!

- "For I know the plans I have for you," declares the Lord, "plans to prosper you and not to harm you, plans to give you hope and a future" (Jeremiah 29:11, NIV).

- Follow them and people will follow you (John C. Maxwell).

- I can do all this through him who gives me strength

(Philippians 4:13, NIV).

- With the crowd dispersed, he climbed the mountain so he could be by himself and pray. He stayed there alone, late into the night (Matthew 14:23, MSG).

Acknowledgments

Husband

I love you and appreciate you for pushing me to get my Master's Degree and for pushing me to complete this book. Even though I would look annoyed when you would ask, "Have you written in your book today," LOL; I appreciate you for the push and for loving me unconditionally.

Mom & Dad

To my parents, I am grateful for the love you taught me. As I grew older and in God, I was taught that love is learned. I am so blessed that God chose you both to be my teachers of love. I put my heart into everything I do because of the love you all showed me. I dedicate this book to you both because you taught me always to be a Leader. Well, Mom and Dad, it paid off. I miss you both immensely.

Bonus Mom

Ever since I can remember, you have been there for me and have played an instrumental part in my life. I know you are always one phone call away. A bonus is considered a reward or getting something extra for doing something good. BJ, you have truly been a BONUS in my life, and I don't know what I did to deserve you. I thank you so much for always being in my corner and treating me like one of your own.

Granny

Granny, your strength has always amazed me. I am grateful for your love and everything you taught me. I remember as a kid you would always remind us "It cost to be the Boss!" Well, Granny the older I got, this same quote I found humorous as a kid, I've found truth in it as an adult. As a Leader, I learned, "It is a cost to being the Boss." I love you and honor you, Granny.

Popa

When I thought life was over for me after losing both parents, it was you who picked me up, took me in, and showed me the love I needed. Popa, from a small girl to a woman, I remember you always being there for me. I dedicate this book to you for all the ways you pushed me and helped in making me the woman I am today. I miss you immensely.

Uncle

Uncle, often I don't know where I'd be without you. You stepped up in my life right in the nick of time and have never left my side. To the man who walked in negative 15 degrees to help start my car. To the man who walked me down the aisle on my wedding day. To the man who makes me laugh and annoyed at the same time. I thank you for the imprint you have made on my life.

My Siblings & Cousin-Siblings

To my siblings and cousins who have always been like siblings to me. I love you all. Thank you for putting up with my "bossy ways" even though I knew you all were tired of me bossing you all around, *LOL*! You allowed me to shine my light and be authentically me. I soon learned that my 'bossy ways" were because I was chosen to raise other Leaders. Can you forgive me for always wanting us to match for family events, crying when people arrived late, and always being a planner and wanting an itinerary? I'm tickled but y'all know I'm serious. God was building my organization and management skills.

My circle of friends

To my circle of friends, you all know exactly who you are, my Sister/Friends. Thank you for allowing me to call and text you to express my emotions throughout my first professional leadership role. Thank you for texting back and forth with encouraging words. Answered my phone calls on my ride to and from my work day to process and when I wanted to throw in the towel. Thank you for reminding me of God's promises for my life. If you had not been there listening to me and more importantly, refocusing my attention on the assignment and calling for my life, I wouldn't have been able to complete this book. Thank you for being my unpaid therapist.

My Village

I dedicate this book to everyone who helped push me spiritually and naturally. My first spiritual home Kingdom of Christ Church (KOC), My training center The Life Church (TLC), Many Godparents, Aunties, Uncles, Siblings, Cousins, Friends, Nieces, and Nephews. I wrote my first book because I knew a village was rooting and pushing me toward being a better version of myself.

I wish you were here, In Loving Memory

Mrs. Kimberly A. Price-Hogan (Mom)

Derrick L. Williams Sr. (Dad)

Lester G. Price (Popa)

Rose Williams (Grandma)

About the Author
Author | Entrepreneur | Leader

Destonie Bell was the bossy classmate, friend, and family member growing up. It was not until two years ago that she realized it was *the Leader* stuck on the inside of her body, waiting to burst out and mature. She began taking classes, receiving mentorship, attending events, and reading books because the leader that was trying to get out would not let her rest until she put in some work.

Destonie's mentor told her, "Whatever breaks your heart is probably the very thing you were created for and purposed."

After years of being under poor leadership, she knew this issue was a heartbreaker for her. It was a nuisance. Everything that was done without considering the team, caused her literal heartaches. In dysfunctional leadership, she began to find her purpose and began to understand her assignment—to inspire growth in emerging leaders.

Destonie holds a Master's in Public Administration. She served as Women's Ministry Lead for six years. Assistant Dean of Operations for two years, Dean of Operations for two years year, and held a partnership in a t-shirt line.

She was born and nurtured for purpose in Chicago, Illinois.

Destonie is passionate about serving in her home as a devoted wife. And an ecstatic mommy-to-be!

An Author, Business Owner, and Leader, she is a change agent chosen to inspire leaders to be competent and confident, influencing positive change while serving others.

Leadership changes when I am called. —Destonie Bell

Let's Stay In Touch

Loved the book? Have feedback for me? Or do you need further support?

I'd love to hear from you. **Contact me @** www.desslead.com

Please leave a review on **Amazon** today. It helps other emerging leaders find my book.

Thank you for your support!

Destonie Bell

DESTONIE BELL

DESSLEAD.COM

1. Hunkins, A. (2022, June). 4 keys to improving your communication. Retrieve from https://www.forbes.com/sites/alainhunkins/2022/06/14/4-keys-to-improving-your-communication/?sh=5d471cd438d9

2. Hunkins, A. (2022, June). 4 keys to improving your communication. Retrieve from https://www.forbes.com/sites/alainhunkins/2022/06/14/4-keys-to-improving-your-communication/?sh=5d471cd438d9

3. Asghar, R. (2020). "Smart Leaders Don't Use Email for The Most Important Things." Retrieved from https://www.forbes.com/sites/robasghar/2020/02/15/its-ok-millennial-leaders-the-phone-is-an-ally-not-an-enemy/?sh=1cd2f65b503c

4. Mcmillan, R., Patterson, K., Switzler, A., et al. (2021). Crucial Conversations: Learn the key skills of talking, listening, and acting together.

5. Mcmillan, R., Patterson, K., Switzler, A., et al. (2021). Crucial Conversations: Learn the key skills of talking, listening, and acting together.

6. Spacey, J. (2018, July). 7 types of relationship building. Retrieved from https://simplicable.com/new/relationship-building

7. Spacey, J. (2018, July). 7 types of relationship building. Retrieved from https://simplicable.com/new/relationship-building

8. Korn, J. (2021, June). Why small talk is anything but small. Retrieved from https://www.forbes.com/sites/juliawuench/2021/06/21/why-small-talk-is-anything-but-small/?sh=746403eb78b0

9. Korn, J. (2021, June). Why small talk is anything but small. Retrieved from https://www.forbes.com/sites/juliawuench/2021/06/21/why-small-talk-is-anything-but-small/?sh=746403eb78b0

10. Korn, J. (2021, June). Why small talk is anything but small. Retrieved from https://www.forbes.com/sites/juliawuench/2021/06/21/why-small-talk-is-anything-but-small/?sh=746403eb78b0

11. Korn, J. (2021, June). Why small talk is anything but small. Retrieved from https://www.forbes.com/sites/juliawuench/2021/06/21/why-small-talk-is-anything-but-small/?sh=746403eb78b0

12. Chapman, Gary D., White, Paul E. (2012, September 1). The 5 Languages of Appreciation in the Workplace: Empowering Organizations by Encouraging People. Chicago, Northfield Pub White.

13. Chapman, Gary D., White, Paul E. (2012, September 1). The 5 Languages of Appreciation in the Workplace: Empowering Organizations by Encouraging People. Chicago, Northfield Pub White.

14. Maxwell, J. (2003). Relationships 101: What every leader needs to know.

15. Powell, B. (2002, October). A three-step process to instill positive accountability with your team. Retrieve from https://www.forbes.com/sites/forbescoachescouncil/2022/10/24/a-three-step-process-to-instill-positive-accountability-with-your-team/?sh=4fbb480563b1

16. Casper, T. (2020, October). "5 Tips to keep burnout at bay." Retrieved from https://www.mayoclinichealthsystem.org/hometown-health/speaking-of-health/5-tips-to-keep-burnout-at-bay

17. Noble Schools, Core Values, https://nobleschools.org/core-values/

18. Powell, B. (2002, October). A three-step process to instill positive accountability with your team. Retrieve from https://www.forbes.com/sites/forbescoachescouncil/2022/10/24/a-three-step-process-to-instill-positive-accountability-with-your-team/?sh=4fbb480563b1

19. Baker, C. (2022). 7 types of feedback for the workplace (and one to avoid). Retrieved https://leaders.com/articles/business/types-of-feedback/

20. Baker, C. (2022). 7 types of feedback for the workplace (and one to avoid). Retrieved https://leaders.com/articles/business/types-of-feedback/

21. Baker, C. (2022). 7 types of feedback for the workplace (and one to avoid). Retrieved https://leaders.com/articles/business/types-of-feedback/

22. Berinato, S. (2018). "Negative feedback rarely leads to improvement." Retrieve from https://hbr.org/2018/01/negative-feedback-rarely-leads-to-improvement

23. Johnson, A. and Ludema, J. (2019). 5 Essentials differences between Criticism and Feedback. Retrieved from https://www.forbes.com/sites/amberjohnson-jimludema/2019/11/07/criticism-vs-feedback/?sh=3a95beff794a

24. Brearley, B. (2016). Why leaders must push back and say "no." Retrieve from https://www.thoughtfulleader.com/push-back-for-leaders/

25. Dorner, U. (2022). What makes a great leader? Best practices when discovering your management style. Retrieved from https://www.forbes.com/sites/forbesbusinesscouncil/2022/02/15/what-makes-a-great-leader-best-practices-when-discovering-your-management-style/?sh=21f234f4246f

26. Dorner, U. (2022). What makes a great leader? Best practices when discovering your management style. Retrieved from https://www.forbes.com/sites/forbesbusinesscouncil/2022/02/15/what-makes-a-great-leader-best-practices-when-discovering-your-management-style/?sh=21f234f4246f

27. Maxwell, John C., 1947 - The five levels of leadership: proven steps to maximize your potential /John C. Maxwell. - 1st ed.

28. Cain, C. (2022, March 27). 9 Ways to Become a Better Team Leader [Instagram Post]. Retrieved October 7, 2022, https://www.instagram.com/p/Cbn3XA6P7-j/?utm_medium=copy_link

29. "Achievement Orientation - Key Step Media". Key Step Media - Leadership, Mindfulness, Emotional Intelligence, 2022, https://www.keystepmedia.com/achievement-orientation/

30. Maxwell, John C., 1947 - The 21 irrefutable laws of leadership: follow them and people will follow you/John C. Maxwell. - 10th anniversary ed.

31. Maxwell, John C., 1947 - The 21 irrefutable laws of leadership: follow them and people will follow you/John C. Maxwell. - 10th anniversary ed.

32. https://www.merriam-webster.com/dictionary/game-changer

www.ingramcontent.com/pod-product-compliance
Lightning Source LLC
Chambersburg PA
CBHW070601170426
43201CB00012B/1896